T0088414

CONTENTS

			Page
1	Choral	BACH	*2*
2	A Distant Land	SCHUMANN	*4*
3	Minuet in G	PURCELL	*5*
4	An Old French Song	TCHAIKOWSKY	*6*
5	The Blacksmith	BRAHMS	*7*
6	March (from *Flavius*)	HANDEL	*8*
7	A Trifle (*Le Petit-rien*)	COUPERIN	*9*
8	Innocence	HAYDN	*10*
9	Chaconne	HANDEL	*12*
10	The Merry Peasant	SCHUMANN	*13*
11	Wiegenlied (*Lullaby*)	MOZART (Bernhard Flies)	*14*
12	Serenade (*An den Mond*)	SCHUBERT	*15*
13	Ecossaise	BEETHOVEN	*16*

NOTE

By using open strings, all the pieces in this album, except *Innocence* (Haydn), may be played in the first position. Some small liberties have been taken in one or two of the melodies so that unduly awkward technical problems might be avoided.

W.F.

EASY CLASSICS FOR THE CELLO

Book 1

Arranged by
WATSON FORBES

1. CHORAL

Harmonised by
J. S. BACH (1685-1750)

Extra cello parts are on sale

© Oxford University Press 1959

Printed in Great Britain
OXFORD UNIVERSITY PRESS, MUSIC DEPARTMENT, GREAT CLARENDON STREET, OXFORD OX2 6DP

Photocopying this copyright material is ILLEGAL.

mf sonore
mf
cresc.
mf
cresc.
mf
f
mp
f
p
p
ff
ff

2. A DISTANT LAND (Op. 15, No. 1.)

(In der Fremde)

from 'Scenes of Childhood'

R. SCHUMANN (1810-56)

3. MINUET IN G

H. PURCELL (1659-95)

Allegretto (♩ = 120)

p
cresc.
p
cresc.
mf
mf
f
f

4. AN OLD FRENCH SONG (Op. 39, No. 16)

from 'Album for the Young'

P. TCHAIKOWSKY (1840-93)

5. THE BLACKSMITH (Op. 19, No. 4)

(Der Schmied)

J. BRAHMS (1833-97)

6. MARCH

from 'Flavius'

G. F. HANDEL (1685-1759)

EASY CLASSICS FOR THE CELLO

Book 1

Arranged by
WATSON FORBES

CELLO

1. CHORAL

Harmonised by
J. S. BACH (1685-1750)

Lento (♩ = 52)

mf *mf* *mf* *p* *mf* *mf sonore* *cresc.* *mf* *f* *mp* *p* *ff*

2. A DISTANT LAND (Op. 15, No. 1.)

(In der Fremde)
from 'Scenes of Childhood'

R. SCHUMANN (1810-56)

Andantino (♩ = 63)

p *mf più agitato* *rit.* *pp a tempo* *cresc.* *mf* *dim.* *pp*

3. MINUET IN G

H. PURCELL (1659-95)

Allegretto (♩ = 120)

p *cresc.* *mf* *f*

© Oxford University Press 1959
Printed in Great Britain
OXFORD UNIVERSITY PRESS, MUSIC DEPARTMENT, GREAT CLARENDON STREET, OXFORD OX2 6DP
Photocopying this copyright material is ILLEGAL.

4. AN OLD FRENCH SONG (Op. 39, No. 16)

from 'Album for the Young'

P. TCHAIKOWSKY (1840-93)

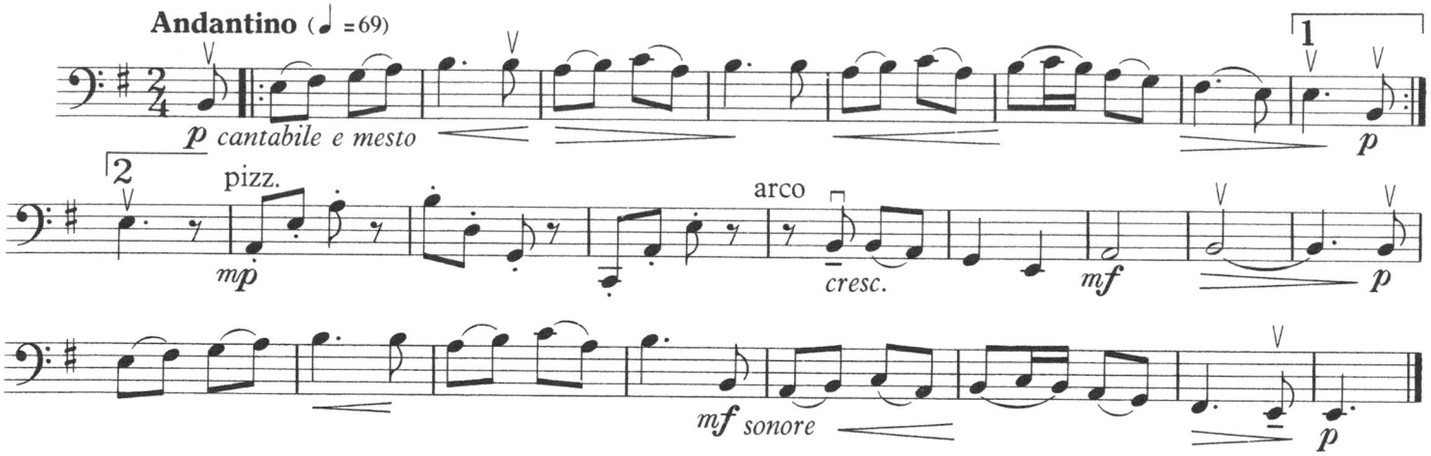

5. THE BLACKSMITH (Op. 19, No. 4)

(Der Schmied)

J. BRAHMS (1833-97)

6. MARCH

from 'Flavius'

G. F. HANDEL (1685-1759)

7. A TRIFLE

(Le Petit-rien)

F. COUPERIN (1668-1733)

continued on next page

8. INNOCENCE

from Op. 53, No. 1

J. HAYDN (1732-1809)

9. CHACONNE

G. F. HANDEL (1685-1759)

10. THE MERRY PEASANT (Op. 68, No. 10)

from 'Album for the Young'

R. SCHUMANN (1810-56)

11. WIEGENLIED (Lullaby)

W. A. MOZART-BERNHARD FLIES *

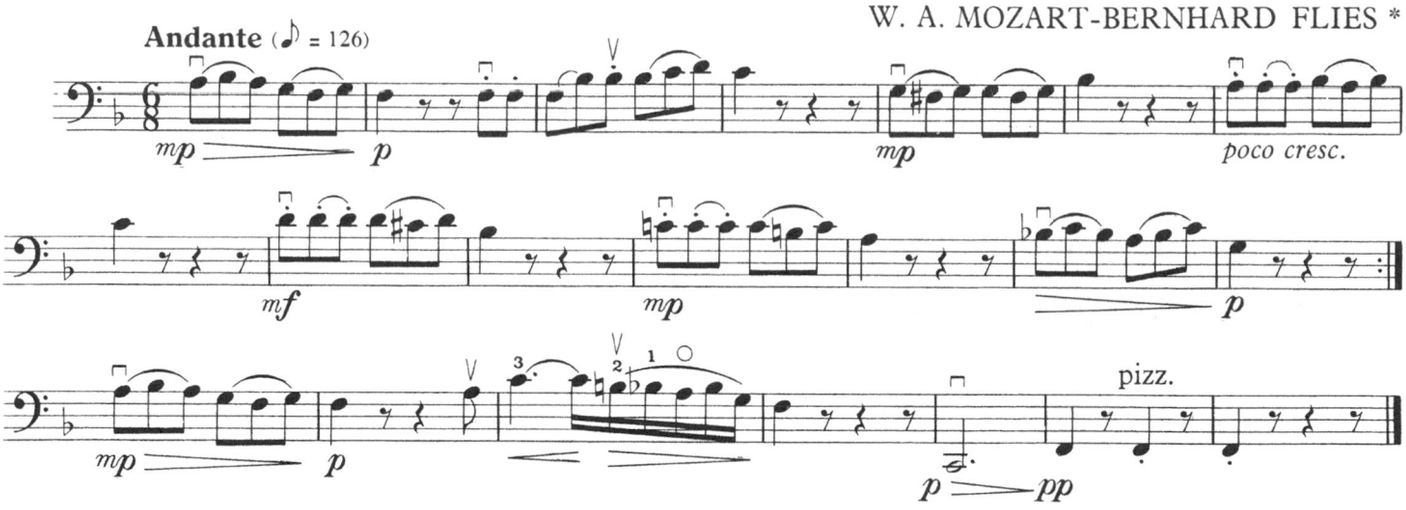

12. SERENADE

(An den Mond)

F. SCHUBERT (1797-1828)

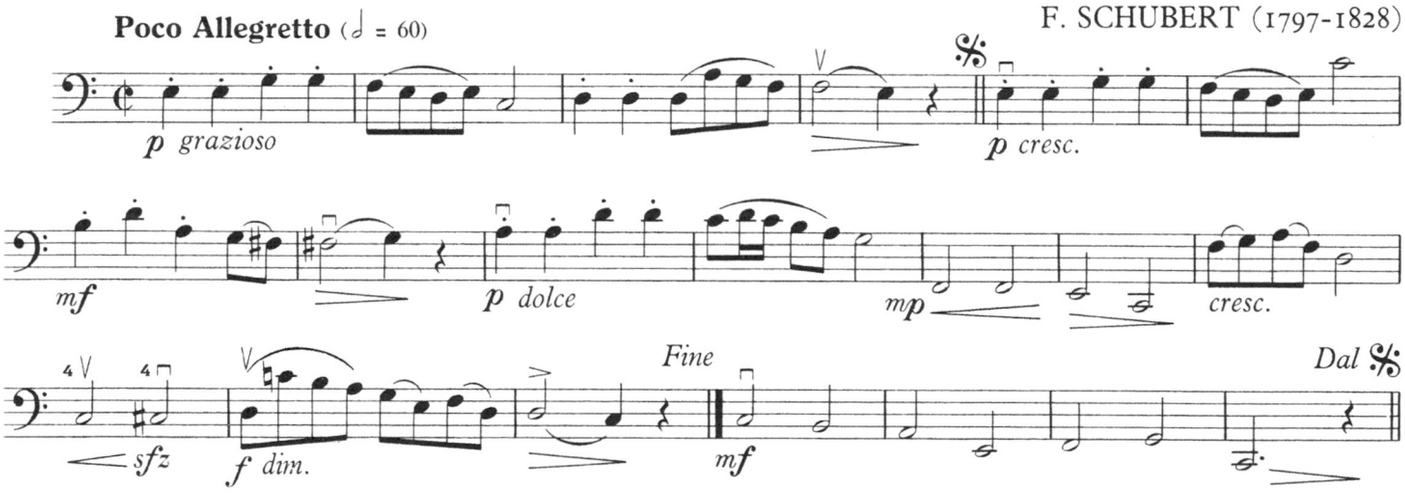

13. ECOSSAISE

L. van BEETHOVEN (1770-1827)

* Well known as a song by Mozart, this Wiegenlied is now known to be the composition of Bernhard Flies

Processed and printed by
Halstan & Co. Ltd., Amersham, Bucks., England

OXFORD UNIVERSITY PRESS

7. A TRIFLE

(Le Petit-rien)

F. COUPERIN (1668-1733)

8. INNOCENCE

from Op. 53, No. 1

J. HAYDN (1732-1809)

Andante (quasi Allegretto) (♪ = 132)

pizz.
p
p
arco
cresc.
f
poco rit.
p
cresc.
f
poco rit.
a tempo
sfz
p
a tempo
p
sfz
p
cresc.
mf
dim. e rit.
p
cresc.
mf
dim. e rit.
p

9. CHACONNE

G. F. HANDEL (1685-1759)

10. THE MERRY PEASANT (Op. 68, No. 10)

from 'Album for the Young'

R. SCHUMANN (1810-56)

11. WIEGENLIED (Lullaby)

W. A. MOZART-BERNHARD FLIES *

* Well known as a song by Mozart, this Wiegenlied is now known to be the composition of Bernhard Flies

12. SERENADE

(An den Mond)

F. SCHUBERT (1797-1828)

13. ECOSSAISE

L. van BEETHOVEN (1770-1827)

Processed and printed by
Halstan & Co. Ltd., Amersham, Bucks., England